INDEPENDENCE DAY

JILL FORAN

www.av2books.com

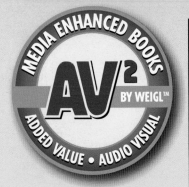

AV² provides enriched content that supplements and complements this book. Weigl's AV² books strive to create inspired learning and engage young minds in a total learning experience.

Your AV² Media Enhanced books come alive with...

Audio
Listen to sections of the book read aloud.

Key Words
Study vocabulary, and complete a matching word activity.

Video
Watch informative video clips.

Quizzes
Test your knowledge.

Go to www.av2books.com, and enter this book's unique code.

Embedded Weblinks
Gain additional information for research.

Slide Show
View images and captions, and prepare a presentation.

BOOK CODE

H 2 1 4 7 4

AV² by Weigl brings you media enhanced books that support active learning.

Try This!
Complete activities and hands-on experiments.

... and much, much more!

Published by AV² by Weigl
350 5th Avenue, 59th Floor
New York, NY 10118
Website: www.av2books.com   www.weigl.com

Library of Congress Control Number: 2012941023

ISBN 978-1-61913-864-3 (hardcover)

ISBN 978-1-61913-867-4 (softcover)

Printed in the United States of America in North Mankato, Minnesota

1 2 3 4 5 6 7 8 9 0 16 15 14 13 12

062012
WEP170512

Editor Heather Kissock   **Design** Terry Paulhus

Weigl acknowledges Getty Images as its primary image supplier for this book.

Every reasonable effort has been made to trace ownership and to obtain permission to reprint copyright material. The publishers would be pleased to have any errors or omissions brought to their attention so that they may be corrected in subsequent printings.

CONTENTS

What Is Independence Day?

Americans celebrate Independence Day on the fourth of July. The United States was born on July 4, 1776. The country's leaders **adopted** a document called the Declaration of Independence on that day. The document said that America was no longer under the control of the **British Crown**. After America's victory in the **Revolutionary War**, America became an independent country. The American people were free.

✷ Many people wear red, white, and blue clothing on Independence Day to show their pride in being American.

Independence Day is America's birthday party. Americans celebrate this birthday in many different ways. They have picnics, watch parades, and spend time with family and friends. Children often wave small flags at the parades. People hold large celebrations with fireworks and music. Most importantly, they celebrate their independence and freedom.

Special Events
THROUGHOUT THE YEAR

RAMADAN
THE EXACT DATES VARY FROM YEAR TO YEAR. IT IS ALWAYS THE NINTH MONTH OF THE MUSLIM CALENDAR.

JANUARY 1
NEW YEAR'S DAY

FEBRUARY (THIRD MONDAY)
PRESIDENTS' DAY

MARCH 17
ST. PATRICK'S DAY

SUNDAY IN MARCH OR APRIL
EASTER

MAY (LAST MONDAY)
MEMORIAL DAY

JUNE 14
FLAG DAY

JULY 4
INDEPENDENCE DAY

SEPTEMBER (FIRST MONDAY)
LABOR DAY

OCTOBER (SECOND MONDAY)
COLUMBUS DAY

NOVEMBER 11
VETERANS DAY

DECEMBER 25
CHRISTMAS DAY

Independence Day History

Until the mid-1500s, only American Indians lived in America. Then, Europeans began to travel to North America. Created in 1607, Virginia was the first permanent British **colony**. Over the next 100 years, 13 colonies were formed in America. The British king ruled over all the colonies from 3,000 miles away.

People in the colonies wanted more freedom. They did not want a king to make their laws or force them to pay taxes. On September 5, 1774, leaders met in Philadelphia. They formed a group called the First Continental Congress. The group sent a list of complaints to the king.

⭐ **Some early European colonists arrived in America on the *Mayflower*.**

King George III did not want to give up control over the colonies. He sent soldiers to the colonies to help control any **rebellion** that might take place. This made the colonists angry. On April 19, 1775, American **patriots** and British soldiers began to fight. The American Revolution had begun. The colonists were fighting for independence from British rule.

In May 1776, the Second Continental Congress met in Philadelphia. The congress decided to write an official statement declaring the separation of the colonies from Great Britain. On June 28, a **committee** of five men presented the first **draft** to congress. The final draft of the Declaration of Independence was adopted on July 4, 1776.

Past and Present Celebrations

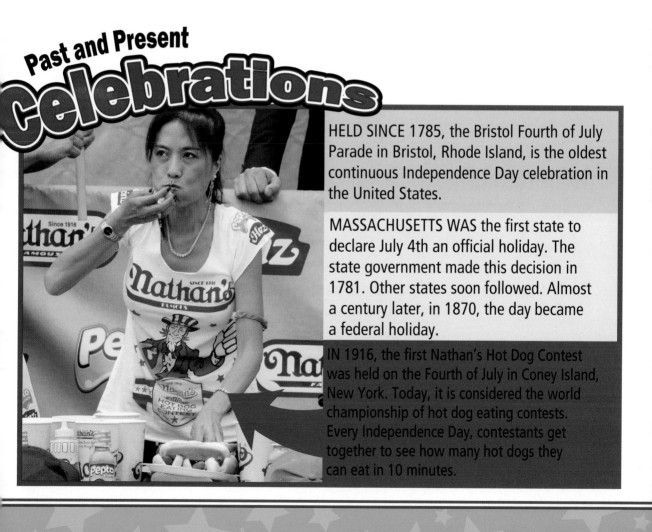

HELD SINCE 1785, the Bristol Fourth of July Parade in Bristol, Rhode Island, is the oldest continuous Independence Day celebration in the United States.

MASSACHUSETTS WAS the first state to declare July 4th an official holiday. The state government made this decision in 1781. Other states soon followed. Almost a century later, in 1870, the day became a federal holiday.

IN 1916, the first Nathan's Hot Dog Contest was held on the Fourth of July in Coney Island, New York. Today, it is considered the world championship of hot dog eating contests. Every Independence Day, contestants get together to see how many hot dogs they can eat in 10 minutes.

Important People

John Adams was one of the **Founding Fathers**. He helped write the Declaration of Independence. He also became the second president of the United States.

Writing the Declaration of Independence was not an easy task. The document had to be very clear. All Americans had to agree with it. The five men who had to draft the document were Benjamin Franklin, John Adams, Roger Sherman, Robert R. Livingston, and Thomas Jefferson. After the Declaration of Independence was adopted, it was distributed to the public. The colonists cherished it as a sign of their liberty.

⭐ **The Declaration of Independence was published in newspapers so the American people could read it.**

John Adams later served as George Washington's vice president. In 1796, Washington **retired**. Adams and Thomas Jefferson both entered the election for president. Adams won the election by three votes. He became the first president to live in the White House, which has been the official home for all presidents since. Adams wrote many letters to Jefferson after they both served as president. Both men died on July 4, 1826.

⭐ **John Adams was one of the first people to suggest that America should be independent.**

First-hand Account

"We hold these truths to be self-evident, that all men are created equal, that they are endowed by their creator with certain unalienable Rights, that among these are Life, Liberty and the pursuit of Happiness."

—*from the second paragraph of the Declaration of Independence*

Independence Day Celebrations

Once independence was officially declared, Americans wanted to celebrate. Crowds gathered at Independence Square in Philadelphia. The Declaration of Independence was read to the public for the first time on July 8, 1776. Bells rang out, music played, and people cheered.

⭐ On Monday, July 8, the Declaration of Independence was read to the public by Colonel John Nixon at the State House in Philadelphia.

The Liberty Bell, located in Philadelphia, Pennsylvania, is a symbol of American independence. It originally cracked when first rung after arrival in Philadelphia.

On July 4, 1777, exactly 1 year after the declaration was adopted, another celebration was held in Philadelphia. This time, crowds gathered to honor the birthday of their nation. They marked the occasion by firing cannons, lighting firecrackers, and dancing.

Fourth of July celebrations spread to other cities and towns. Americans wanted to honor the day they gained their independence from Great Britain. By the mid-1800s, everyone was celebrating Independence Day.

Independence Around the World

CANADA

Canada Day, July 1, celebrates **Confederation** with outdoor parades, carnivals, festivals, barbecues, air and water shows, fireworks, and free musical concerts.

NORWAY

Norwegian Constitution Day is celebrated on May 17 with children's parades that have flags, marching bands, signs, and greetings from the royal family.

ITALY

There is no Independence Day in Italy, but June 2 is "Festa della Repubblica" ("Republic Day"), which celebrates when Italy became a **republic** on June 2, 1946.

Celebrating Today

Today, Americans celebrate Independence Day in many ways. People do not have to work so they have time to spend with their families. They attend picnics and eat summer foods. They also take part in holiday events, such as baseball games, three-legged races, and pie-eating contests. Many communities host Independence Day parades. During these parades, crowds of people line the streets. They wave American flags as marching bands and beautiful **floats** pass them by.

After the Sun goes down on Independence Day, people gather to watch the fireworks displays. Most cities and towns across the United States set off fireworks on the Fourth of July.

⭐ On Independence Day, many people celebrate by grilling traditional American foods, such as hot dogs and hamburgers.

Many cities and towns, including Boston, hold outdoor concerts as part of their Independence Day celebrations. These celebrations often end with fireworks displays.

⭐ The American flag is an important part of celebrations in Washington, D.C., and other cities in the United States.

Independence Day in the United States

Independence Day is celebrated across the country. This map shows a few celebrations that take place every year.

OKLAHOMA The people of Edmond, Oklahoma, celebrate Independence Day with a festival called LibertyFest. This one-week festival features a Fourth of July parade, a car show, and kite competitions.

ARIZONA
In Flagstaff, Arizona, American Indians celebrate Independence Day with a 3-day powwow. The powwow includes traditional dancing, drumming, and a rodeo.

Arizona

Oklahoma

Hawai'i

0   970 Miles

Alaska

0   1,278 Miles

ALASKA
Hundreds of people in Seward, Alaska, celebrate the Fourth of July by taking part in a 6-mile foot race. Racers try to make it to the top of Mount Marathon and back in less than one hour.

NEW YORK In New York City, Macy's July 4 fireworks display lights up the sky over the Hudson River. Its "Golden Mile" fireworks feature a shower of golden sparks stretching 1 mile across the river.

New York

Pennsylvania

PENNSYLVANIA In Philadelphia, Pennsylvania, crowds gather to take part in the Freedom Festival at Independence Hall. Actors dress up like America's early leaders. They read the Declaration of Independence to the crowd.

Washington, D.C.

WASHINGTON, D.C. The National Independence Day Parade draws the attention of Americans to the real meaning of the holiday. The flag is the center of the celebration of this patriotic day in the nation's capital.

N
W—E
S

0   207 Miles

Independence Day Symbols

Many people think of parades, fireworks, picnics, and summer holidays when they think of Independence Day. Independence Day is more than parades and fireworks, however. The holiday is a special celebration of freedom. Many national symbols help remind Americans of their freedom.

THE AMERICAN FLAG

All over the country, Americans wave the flag at Fourth of July parades. The design of the first flag had seven red stripes, six white stripes, and thirteen stars on a blue field. The flag still has thirteen stripes for the original colonies. Stars have been added to the flag as new states join the union. Today, the flag has 50 stars.

THE LIBERTY BELL

The Liberty Bell was hung in the Philadelphia State House tower in 1753. On July 8, 1776, it rang to celebrate the adoption of the Declaration of Independence. In 1777, it rang to mark the first Independence Day celebration. It is now at the Liberty Bell Center in Philadelphia.

THE STATUE OF LIBERTY

The Statue of Liberty, a gift to the United States from France, stands in New York City. Her right hand holds a torch that stands for liberty. In her left hand is a **tablet** with the date July 4, 1776. People visit the Statue of Liberty to celebrate our freedom.

A Song to Remember

"The Star-Spangled Banner" is a song that is often heard on Independence Day. It helps people remember the ideals behind the founding of the United States of America. Here are all eight verses of the song:

Oh, say can you see
by the dawn's early light

What so proudly we hailed
at the twilight's last gleaming?

Whose broad stripes and bright stars
through the perilous fight,

O'er the ramparts we watched
were so gallantly streaming?

And the rocket's red glare,
the bombs bursting in air,

Gave proof through the night
that our flag was still there.

Oh, say does that star-spangled
banner yet wave

O'er the land of the free
and the home of the brave?

- Francis Scott Key

Write Your Own Song

Songwriting is a fun way to express thoughts and ideas. Get creative, and write your own song.

Listen to a song that you like, and pay attention to the words. Which words rhyme? How many verses are there? How many lines are in each verse? How many times is the chorus sung?

Start brainstorming ideas. What do you want your song to be about? Choose an event, idea, person, or feeling you would like to write about.

Write the verses. Songs usually have three or four verses. Each one will be different but should relate to the chorus.

Think of a tune for your song. Some songwriters like to write the tune before the words. Others will write them at the same time.

Write the chorus to your song. The chorus is the main idea of the song. It connects the verses together.

Many songwriters work with other people to create songs. Try working with a classmate or friend to think of a tune or words for your song.

19

Making a Craft Stick Flag

This easy-to-make flag is not truly authentic, but it is a fun way for children to learn about the colors and formation of the American flag.

Craft sticks

Paintbrush

Sticker stars

Red, white, and blue paint

Glue

Cardboard

Hole punch

Yarn

5 Easy Steps to Complete Your Stick Flag

1. Paint six craft sticks red and five sticks white.

2. Glue these in place on a piece of cardboard, alternating the red and white sticks.

3. Paint a square of blue in the upper left corner.

4. Place sticker stars in the blue block.

5. To hang, punch two holes in the top of the cardboard and thread a piece of yarn for the hanger.

Make an Independence Day Shake

Ingredients

2 cups milk
vanilla ice cream
1 can of whipped
   cream
blue food coloring

ice cubes
red cherries with stems
red, white, and
    blue sprinkles

Equipment

Ice cream scoop
Blender

Directions

1. With an adult's help, put 2 scoops of ice cream and 2 cups of milk in the blender. Blend for 30 seconds.
2. Add two ice cubes and a few drops of blue food coloring to the mixture. Blend for another 30 seconds.
3. Pour the mixture into a tall, clear glass. Add whipped cream, sprinkles, and a cherry to the top of the shake.
4. Enjoy your red, white, and blue ice cream shake.

Test Your Knowledge!

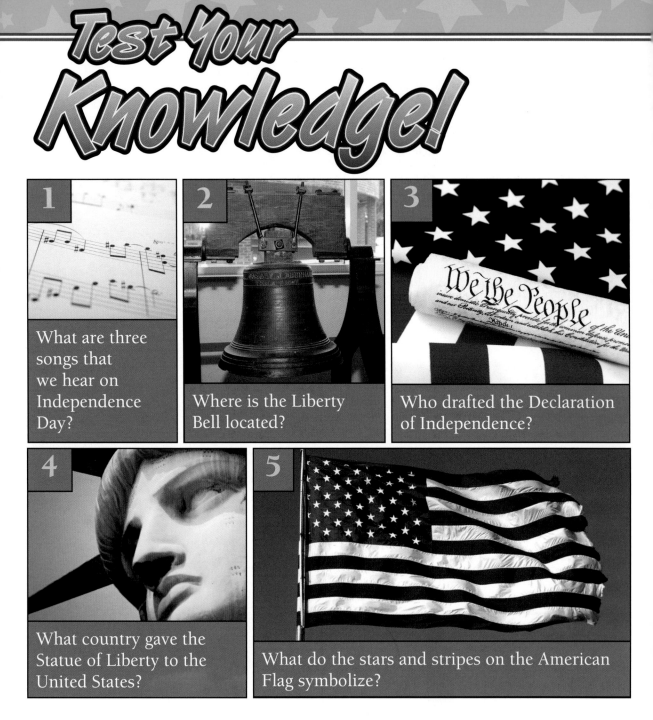

1
What are three songs that we hear on Independence Day?

2
Where is the Liberty Bell located?

3
Who drafted the Declaration of Independence?

4
What country gave the Statue of Liberty to the United States?

5
What do the stars and stripes on the American Flag symbolize?

Quiz Answers:
1. "The Star-Spangled Banner," "God Bless America," and "America the Beautiful"
2. Philadelphia, Pennsylvania
3. John Adams, Benjamin Franklin, Robert R. Livingston, Thomas Jefferson, and Roger Sherman
4. France
5. The stars symbolize the fifty states, and the stripes represent the original 13 colonies

Key Words

adopted: accepted as official

British Crown: the government of Great Britain, ruled by a king or queen

colony: a territory ruled by another country

committee: a group that is formed to act on something

draft: an early form of a written document

floats: low, flat platforms on wheels in parades

Founding Fathers: men who led the American Revolution

patriots: people who love their country

rebellion: fighting against the rule of another country

republic: a government in which people elect their leaders

retired: to stop working

Revolutionary War: the war between Great Britain and the United States that led to America's independence

tablet: pad of paper

Index

Log on to www.av2books.com

AV² by Weigl brings you media enhanced books that support active learning. Go to www.av2books.com, and enter the special code found on page 2 of this book. You will gain access to enriched and enhanced content that supplements and complements this book. Content includes video, audio, weblinks, quizzes, a slide show, and activities.

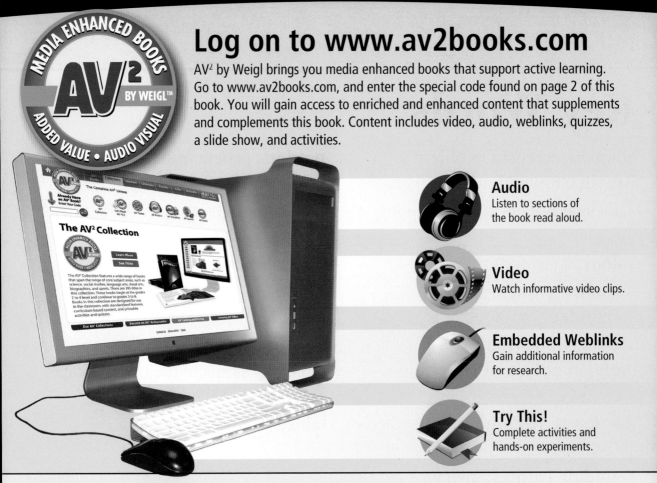

Audio
Listen to sections of the book read aloud.

Video
Watch informative video clips.

Embedded Weblinks
Gain additional information for research.

Try This!
Complete activities and hands-on experiments.

WHAT'S ONLINE?

Try This!	Embedded Weblinks	Video	EXTRA FEATURES
Pages 8-9 Write a biography about an important person.	**Pages 6-7** Find out more about the history of Independence Day.	**Pages 4-5** Watch a video about Independence Day.	**Audio** Listen to sections of the book read aloud.
Pages 10-11 Describe the features and special events of a similar celebration around the world.	**Pages 10-11** Learn more about similar celebrations around the world.	**Pages 12-13** Check out a video about how people celebrate Independence Day.	**Key Words** Study vocabulary, and complete a matching word activity.
Pages 14-15 Complete a mapping activity about Independence Day celebrations.	**Pages 16-17** Find information about important holiday symbols.		**Slide Show** View images and captions, and prepare a presentation.
Pages 16-17 Try this activity about important holiday symbols.	**Pages 18-19** Link to more information about Independence Day.		
Pages 20-21 Play an interactive activity.	**Pages 20-21** Check out more holiday craft ideas.		**Quizzes** Test your knowledge.

AV² was built to bridge the gap between print and digital. We encourage you to tell us what you like and what you want to see in the future.
Sign up to be an AV² Ambassador at www.av2books.com/ambassador.